HOW STEM BUILT EMPIRES™

HOW STEM BUILT THE INCAN EMPIRE

MICHAEL HESSEL-MIAL

Rosen YA™
New York

Published in 2020 by The Rosen Publishing Group, Inc.
29 East 21st Street, New York, NY 10010

First Edition

Library of Congress Cataloging-in-Publication Data

Names: Hessel-Mial, Michael, author.
Title: How STEM built the Incan empire / Michael Hessel-Mial. Description: First edition. | New York : Rosen Publishing, 2020. | Series: How STEM built empires | Audience: Grades: 7–12. | Includes bibliographical references and index.
Identifiers: LCCN 2019013256| ISBN 9781725341470 (library bound) | ISBN 9781725341463 (pbk.)
Subjects: LCSH: Science—Peru—History—Juvenile literature. | Technology—Peru—History—Juvenile literature. | Engineering—Peru—History—Juvenile literature. | Mathematics—Peru—History—Juvenile literature. | Incas—Mathematics—Juvenile literature. | Incas—History—Juvenile literature.
Classification: LCC Q127.P4 H47 2020 | DDC 509.85/09024—dc23
LC record available at https://lccn.loc.gov/2019013256

Manufactured in the United States of America

On the cover: Incan ruins like these are among the longest-lasting and most impressive structures in the Americas.

CONTENTS

INTRODUCTION

To anyone who has studied world civilizations, a few features of organized society consistently stand out as essential. The wheel is one such important invention. Likewise, it is impossible to imagine a major power without some form of writing for communication. Digging deeper, one might identify a favorable climate, metal tools, or useful pack animals to help people carry things as other essential elements. It is hard to build any civilization—let alone a great one—without these features.

The civilization of the Incas, founded at an undefined date in the thirteenth century, is a significant break in assumptions about most civilizations. This sophisticated society used no wheels or iron; had no friendly climate for growing or travel; and had no writing system resembling those used in other great societies. Yet these mountain-dwelling people built an empire that was the most powerful in South America at the time of European exploration. Spanning the Andes mountain range over thousands of miles, the Incan Empire absorbed smaller cultures in climates ranging from mountain to rain forest to desert, spreading its unique technologies along the way.

The Incas adapted to their environment with remarkable inventions, some borrowed and some

This painting of Manco Capac, legendary founder of the Incan Empire, depicts traditional Incan symbols in a European style.

homegrown, and used them to administer the needs of a mighty state. Struggling to farm the slopes of the mountains of the Andes, the Incas rebuilt the landscape with terrace architecture. They used common-sense hand tools to shape the stones into earthquake-proof buildings and roads. They took advantage of geographic diversity to cultivate and trade a wide variety of crops. They used textiles to produce a form of communication seen nowhere else in the world: the quipu, a system of knotted yarn that conveyed mathematical data—it is still being interpreted by scholars today. By looking at the Incan Empire, it is obvious that the science, technology, engineering, and math (STEM) innovations that civilizations deploy are often shaped by their unique worldview and circumstances.

The Incan Empire created a set of ideas for how society should be ordered, which gave direction and purpose to the STEM its people utilized. Like the Roman Empire—which wanted to spread its unique legal code around the Mediterranean world—the Incas had a complex governing system that linked religion, social order, and the economy. Centered around the sacred capital of Cuzco, every geographic region was given a distinct economic and religious role. As the empire expanded, conquered groups were absorbed into the system, preserving their religious beliefs while accepting the power of Inti, the Incan sun god. In exchange, Incan society took responsibility for caring for each individual in times of need, creating a moneyless society organized with information from the quipu.

Incan civilization, like many other complex societies in the Americas, was conquered and destroyed by European explorers in the sixteenth century. As a result of this destruction, scholars in modern times are left with the task of reconstructing this civilization. By sifting through archaeological data, decoding quipus, poring over Spanish chronicles of the Incas, and speaking with Incan descendants still living the old traditions, it is possible to interpret how STEM built the complex Incan world.

CHAPTER ONE

THE "SON OF THE SUN" CREATES AN EMPIRE IN CUZCO

Well before the Incas became an empire, the Andean civilizations were distinctive, developing their unique technologies wit any influence of societies outside the region. Arc 1400 BCE, in the period historians call the Early Horizon, Chavín civilization created religious tradi and weaving techniques that influenced the later Moche and Nazca cultures. During the Middle Ho period (600–1000 CE), the Tiwanaku and Huari established small, influential empires. The Tiwan ruled near Lake Titicaca and developed stone ma imitated by the later Incas. The Huari ruled furthe north, building roads and inventing the quipu. Bo these societies mysteriously disappeared and we replaced by fragmented warring states. Scholars especially curious about these societies' influen on the Incas—the Quechua-speaking valley-dwell who began expanding from their center in Cuzco twelfth century CE.

INCAN ORIGINS: MYTH AND REALITY

Incan legends say that the god Viracocha—son o the sun god Inti—created the Tiwanaku from sto

Shown here is a statue of Pachacuti, the ninth Sapa Inca. Pachacuti is traditionally credited with major land conquests, the design of Cuzco, and the composition of many Incan hymns.

A male-female pair, Manco Capac and Mama Ocllo, were specially chosen from the Tiwanaku to bring the sun cult to the small village of Cuzco. Manco Capac was the Sapa Inca, the name for Incan rulers, and considered the common ancestor of the empire. Manco Capac's heirs are said to have invented terrace agriculture and the *mit'a* system, which was a tax paid in labor rather than money. It was Pachacuti Inca Yupanqui, an emperor whose name meant "earth shaker," who turned the growing Incan state into a full empire at the end of the fifteenth century. He is credited with inventing the empire's core institutions, including the Inti sun cult and ritual calendar, the urban planning of Cuzco, and ritual poems and dances commemorating Incan power.

Of these founding myths, passed along by Spanish chroniclers, only some are true. Pachacuti was indeed a military ruler who helped shape Incan identity and institutions when he took power in 1438. However, the historical early expansion was considerably milder than these myths suggest; the surrounding Colla, Wanka, and Chanca cultures were tiny villages that were absorbed due to Cuzco's growth as an economic power. While surrounding states focused on war, building defensive settlements from 1000 to 1400, the early Incas invested in centrally organizing agricultural production. Expanding output with irrigation and terrace agriculture, the early Incas urbanized and absorbed these smaller neighbors.

The Incas did eventually become a military empire, conquering the stronger Chanca, Sican, and Chimú peoples. The Incas applied their system of

BECOMING INCAN: ABSORBING RIVAL CULTURES

Like many expanding empires, the Incas were confronted with the task of absorbing different populations, with widely varying languages and cultures. The Incas allowed these conquered states to keep their religious traditions—so long as they also worshipped Inti. When conquered people rebelled, the empire used an elaborate system of forced resettlement, called *mitmaqkuna*. Loyal Incan villages would be moved to these new frontiers, while original inhabitants would be uprooted in the thousands and moved to various parts of the empire. As a result of this system, dissenters were unable to organize successfully, limiting their ability to fight back.

Once conquered, these new additions to the empire were treated as full citizens of the state, entitled to its benefits and required to participate in the state-run economy. Conquered states were fully absorbed into the Incan administrative system and often saw their cities rebuilt and connected to the Incan road networks. However, all was not completely stable. By the time of the Spanish arrival in the region in the 1520s, the Incas were devoting a great deal of resources to containing provincial rebellions.

labor organization to amass armies in the tens of thousands. Pachacuti, his son Tupac Yupanqui, and his grandson Huayna Capac all followed a pattern of diplomacy and war. Incan armies would first approach the enemy offering tribute and favorable terms of surrender. If the terms were accepted, the peacefully conquered people would adopt Quechua and become Incan subjects. If the empire encountered resistance, they would attack—almost always successfully.

The Incan army never raised professional soldiers, instead drafting everyday citizens as a part of the labor tax. These soldiers were armed with a range of simple, but impressive, weapons of wood and stone: fire-hardened spears, slings for launching stones, shields, bows and arrows, and wooden swords that were reportedly as sharp as metal. They used their large numbers to intimidate the opposition. The Incas also had superior supply chains, using the road system to transport supplies to enemy territory.

THE IDEAS BEHIND INCAN SOCIAL ORGANIZATION

Incan society had two fundamental concepts that were used to understand the world. The first main concept was a desire for everything to resemble the sun god, Inti. The Incas saw society as organized by a central point radiating out in all directions, just like the sun. The plan for the capital in Cuzco fit this model, with roads and sacred sites structured in lines radiating from the center of the city. Quipus, terraces, and people fit into this system as well, leading to a hierarchical form of organization. The second main concept was the division of all things into two complementary pairs: male and female, light and dark, sun and moon. These pairs would appear in Incan astronomical concepts and in the division of social groups within the empire. Incan STEM deployed these concepts to give structure to the world around the empire.

The fundamental social unit of Incan society was the ayllu, or clan claiming a common ancestor. These clans saw themselves as a large, extended family and practiced collective ownership of goods and land. Each clan's ancestor or direct descendant was also called the Sapa Inca, or "the only Inca." This title was also used in reference to the emperor of the Incas. The ayllus were organized into ritual groups based on location. From these social divisions, the Incan state would compel labor taxes on a strict schedule. The empire conscripted groups in units of ten for public works. This decimal system was also used for warfare.

The Incan Empire did not have a money system. Though valuable goods like precious fabrics and coca leaves were sometimes traded, they were never an official, government-regulated currency. Surrounding cultures did in fact have currencies of their own, such as beads or metal tokens, but none of these were adopted over the course of Incan conquest. Instead, the Incas adopted the mit'a system, in which everyone was compelled to participate. In exchange for contributing labor, people traded agricultural goods from other regions, pottery, textiles, and forged metal objects.

CRAFT TECHNOLOGIES THAT SHAPED THE EMPIRE

The most important Incan craft technologies were pottery, metallurgy, and textiles. Each of these were borrowed from surrounding cultures, fit into the Incan belief system, and expanded into large-scale industries. Incan potters used molds to consistently shape their handmade pieces and decorated them with elaborate geometrical designs. The most distinctive Incan pottery was the aryballos, a large jug with a narrow neck and handles on each side. These handles were used to rope the aryballos to the carrier's back, like a modern backpack, to transport liquids on mountain paths.

The Andean region is rich in gold, silver, copper, and tin, but low in iron. Though early civilizations combined copper and tin into bronze, these materials were primarily used for decorative objects rather than tools. The earlier Moche and later Chimú cultures developed traditions of metal extraction and production that the Incas later utilized. The Moche (100–700 CE) built ceramic furnaces that were specially vented to extract metals from ore and used ceramic and stone molds to cast metals. The Chimú people (900–1470 CE) developed alloy techniques to produce various combinations of silver, gold, and copper. They would hammer the metals into composite sheets that were layered and fused using early soldering techniques. The resulting decorative items were remarkably delicate and precise.

This is an aryballos vessel recovered from Peru's north coast. The crosshatched decorative style is characteristic of Incan ceramics.

As the Incas expanded, they took control of the surrounding mines and metallurgy techniques. The Incas believed that gold was the sweat of the sun, and silver was the tears of the moon. Techniques of alloying were applied to Incan values of complementary pairs and were reproduced in decorative arts across the empire. Larger mines were converted into state enterprises employing hundreds of laborers, digging shafts up to 245 feet (74.7 meters) in length. The Incas allowed the locals to control the smaller mines, which encouraged the ritual exchanges of metal goods between the state and the provinces.

Even more so than important technologies like metallurgy and ceramics, textile production was a significant part of Incan culture, functioning as a social marker and as a luxury good as valuable as gold. Cloth was a vehicle for cultural expression, in which women had a sacred role creating fabric for the state. Textiles were essential components of rituals for every stage of life, from birth to death. The Sapa Inca was crowned with luxurious red fabrics woven in a style reserved for the ruler alone.

Incan fabrics were largely cotton and wool. Weavers used a simple handheld spindle called a *phusca*. Everyday fabrics were known as *huasca*, created primarily for comfort over style. Nobles, however, wore a luxury fabric known as *cumbi*. These fabrics also combined elaborate weaving patterns of a variety of geometrical figures. Specialists also incorporated feathers and gold bangles into their textiles. Rather than creating high fashion, however, these special

An example of the cumbi style of textile worn by nobles, the decorations on this luxurious fabric conveyed detailed information about the wearer's social position.

fabrics were markers of social status and cultural origin. These fabrics were also used in religious sacrifices, and the system of ceremonial exchanges between subservient cultures that was designed to foster loyalty among the Incan subjects. To meet this demand for an enormous range of fabrics, the state designated entire villages to the task, employing hundreds of weavers at a time to produce fabric.

The STEM achievements attributed to Incan society did not necessarily originate with native Incas. Instead, they applied their belief system to give each technology special meaning and new purpose. That allowed the Incas to put those technologies to work, dramatically scaling up production and distribution across the board. The Incas' master technology was their organization, which put every technology into its proper place, leading to innovation and advancement.

CHAPTER TWO

INCAN FARMERS RESHAPE THE LANDSCAPE

The vast territories of the Incan Empire at its height are full of striking contrasts: winding mountains and forbidding deserts, rain forests and seaside coasts, as well as the broad plains of the altiplano. Some farmland in the Andes is—at 13,000 feet (4,000 m)—the highest altitude farming area in the world. These elevated areas were especially vulnerable to frost, which could easily destroy a harvest of crops. In addition, the region was especially vulnerable to the appearance of El Niño, a weather pattern appearing every five to seven years, which caused extreme rains in some areas and droughts in others. However, with the challenges also came opportunity, as the Andes are among the most diverse biomes in the world, allowing Inca agriculturalists to produce a rich, healthy cuisine.

Agricultural needs are a frequent driver for STEM development. Many of the earliest civilizations in the world flourished by experimenting with new crops or creating new planting tools. For the Incas, the fundamental constraints of the landscape encouraged an outlook that worked with the land, putting its challenging characteristics to work. Incan and pre-Incan STEM innovations produced terracing and food production systems that changed the Peruvian landscape—as well as diets around the world.

ROYAL ESTATES TURN TERRACES INTO LAND ART

Other than the great Incan cities of Cuzco and Quito, one of the greatest (and certainly most famous) sites in the Incan Empire is Machu Picchu, a remote walled city high in the mountains. Machu Picchu was intended as a military outpost, royal estate, or a display of Incan power

to the provinces—or likely all three at once. The location boasts some of the best stone masonry, as well as the most elaborate terrace architecture, in the Incan world.

Similar to other royal estates like Choquequirau, Machu Picchu was built to fit elegantly into the landscape; natural features like mountains, the river, and the night sky harmonize with the stone structures and surrounding terrace architecture. Based on measurements of the land area, these terraces would not have produced enough food for the estate's inhabitants. Instead, the terraces are an ambitious display of power and engineering. Machu Picchu is one of many examples of the Incas turning their STEM practices into rich displays of imperial power.

This panoramic image of Machu Picchu shows the scope of the ruins and the celebrated work of Incan architects and builders.

GROWING BY CONSTRAINT

Because such large swaths of Incan territory were taken up by mountainous land, there was a natural—and critical—need to maximize growing area. A bird's-eye view of the Peruvian mountain paths reveals remarkable human-made structures: ribbons of parallel terraces resembling broad staircases on the sides of the mountains. These terraces were built to extend every possible unit of land from the forbidding environment by creating more flat surfaces than would exist naturally. Terracing was a practice in use by Andean civilizations well before the rise of the Inca, and Incan farmers continued to improve terrace designs. As the Incas were expanding their empire, they used mit'a labor to construct an additional 2.5 million acres (1 million hectares) of land.

Along with creating extra area, the terraces created additional advantages. Terraces served as a check against soil erosion, made irrigation simpler to manage, and deepened the soil, which allowed plants to root themselves more securely. The structures also exerted a small measure of control over the local climate. The cold, downward-flowing mountain air would often increase in turbulence as it swept over the jutting steps, limiting the dangers of overnight frost, which could be disastrous for crop growth.

The standard Incan terrace system was constructed of multiple parts. First, laborers would build a retaining wall to hold the soil in, making the face of the step. Then, they would bring in pebbles and soil to fill the terrace. Workers would start by filling the bottom

A royal estate in Inca Písac, located in the Sacred Valley of the Incas, is shown here. The terrace architecture follows the natural incline of the valley slope, as Incan stonework commonly did.

with pebbles, to improve drainage during rains. After, soil would be filled in and leveled, creating a long, narrow strip of new cropland. To help farmers get from one level of the terrace to the next, there were paths running along the sides, or steps built into the retaining walls.

These construction sites were commonly built near a naturally occurring spring, which would be used for irrigating the entire terrace complex. Because the highland springs tended to irregularly flood, the Incas developed different types of canals to irrigate the terraces. A main canal would redirect water from the spring to the terraces, and then a series of horizontal canals would serve each level of the terrace. The horizontal canals were linked by drop canals, which served as artificial waterfalls, allowing water to flow downward from one level to the next.

The most recognizable agricultural terraces are known as bench terraces, built high in the mountains. However, the Incas also used terracing at the bases of the mountains, called valley-bottom terraces. There were fewer constraints on these lower-altitude structures. Their slopes were gentler and the terraces themselves were wider, sometimes not even requiring a retaining wall. The valley-bottom terraces tended to cover larger areas of land with scarcer water resources, so their administration was more strictly administered, while the bench terraces were under more local control. It was typical of Incan civilization to apply the same general structures across the entire empire, with subtle adaptations to fit the specific needs of individual environments.

As a technological development, terracing is a remarkable example of a people altering the local ecology in sophisticated, far-reaching ways. As the Incan and pre-Incan civilizations experimented with these landscapes through a long series of trials and errors, they discovered techniques that fit snugly into the environment. Though terraces are not always as flashy and recognizable as the temples of Cuzco, they reveal fundamental features of the Incan outlook on STEM, and they played a major role in the development of the empire.

AN ASTRONAUT FOOD, INVENTED EARLY

Modern-day visitors to NASA headquarters might learn about freeze-dried food, a type of preserved food eaten during spaceflight. Though the Incas did not have high-tech NASA-issued freeze-dried protein foods, the empire developed chuño, freeze-dried potatoes, and charki, freeze-dried meat.

In making these unique foods, the Incas took advantage of their natural nemesis: the morning frosts. At higher altitudes, frost was a consistent danger to food production, but it had its uses. The Incas would leave potatoes or meat out overnight to freeze, then scrape the frost crystals from the food. After several nights of this process, the food was sufficiently dried out and safe for long-term storage.

Though these freeze-dried items were certainly useful for local consumption, especially in stews, the practice of freeze-drying also served a larger purpose. These goods filled regional storehouses in case of future emergencies. They were also ferried across the empire, proving easier to transport than fresh foods. Such food became staples for soldiers, who ate the dried tubers and jerky during long campaigns.

FARMING PRACTICES AND STAPLE CROPS

Typical Incan farmers had a few relatively standard practices, wherever they were. They would often use simple farming implements, like the *chaquitaclla* foot plow. This agricultural tool had a wooden or bronze blade at the end. It remains in use to this day, and the device accrued cultural significance during the empire, as the Sapa Inca would conduct a yearly ceremony of groundbreaking to start the cycle of planting. In addition to these tools, farmers stayed alert by chewing coca leaves. Though coca is a dangerous stimulant in its purified form, it is relatively mild in its leaf form. Farmers grew collectively as a single ayllu, often tending to strips of land ranging from the valley bottoms to the mountains to maximize crop diversity.

Crops varied by altitude. The primary staple crop of the high-altitude *puna* region was the potato, as well as other tubers like the *oca* and *llucu*. Such tubers can withstand the short days and low temperatures of the region, and due to centuries of selective cultivation, they developed into hundreds of different potato varieties. One of these breeds was very bitter but was freeze-dried into a substance called chuño, a foundation of Andean cuisine. The Incas also cultivated camelid animals, especially llamas and alpacas. These animals provided meat, wool, transportation for goods, and dung for fertilizer.

The Andes are the location of some of the highest-altitude farming of anywhere in the world, with some regions planting tubers at 13,000 feet (4,000 m) above sea level. At this height, only a few kinds of crops can grow—but in the lower altitudes, the Incas cultivated a much wider variety of foods, which added to the Incan diet. In the mid-altitude *quechua* region, the Incas grew maize, quinoa, squash, beans, and chili peppers. Maize was especially important, as it was used in the primary Incan alcohol: chicha. This corn beer had important uses in both rituals and textiles.

In the lower-altitude *yunga* region, the Incas grew manioc root, cotton, and sweet potatoes. Though the climate was milder in these valley bottoms, rainfall was much scarcer, requiring irrigation. However, none of these regions should be seen as separate from the others. The Incan Empire was organized such that

An expanse of potato farmland, still planted and harvested according to traditional Incan practices, is shown here. Even centuries after conquest, much of the terraced land remains uncultivated.

subsistence farming—a system in which farmers grow food for their own survival—was unnecessary. The farming of each of these goods was coordinated by the state, and every worker had a share in the diverse produce of the empire.

Incan agricultural evolution highlights a core feature of the empire's outlook toward STEM: science and technology were advanced in an attempt to meet challenging conditions and turn them into strengths. Incas did so by harnessing collective labor power to transform the landscape. They also used these skills to foster biodiversity, taking advantage of crops in a wide variety of environments to produce a balanced diet. After the Incas made their fateful contact with the Spanish, many Incan staple crops would make their way to every corner of the world, filling bellies with crops born in the Peruvian highlands.

CHAPTER THREE

THE MAGIC OF STONE IN INCAN INFRASTRUCTURE

The most enduring expression of the Incan Empire is in what its people built; the remains of roads, walls, temples, and cities still dot the Peruvian landscape. These structures represent incredible problem-solving skills, having been built using relatively simple tools. A closer look at Incan infrastructure reveals that these structures represent the empire's belief systems, economy, and social structure.

STONE MASONRY: A PRACTICAL EXPRESSION OF INCAN VALUES

Throughout Peru, many walls built by the Incas are still standing today. Just looking at these walls, a number of features stand out. The stone blocks are irregularly shaped, fitting like the pieces of a jigsaw puzzle. The face of each stone bulges slightly outward at the center before tapering into the seams between blocks. Perhaps most importantly, the seams themselves are bonded without mortar. Incan builders deliberately chose this style of construction. One reason is practical: mortar between stones is typically the weak point in a structure, but by cutting the stones to fit together perfectly, Inca masons ensured their walls

Shown here is a typical example of Incan bonded masonry, with its unusual angles and gently bulging stone faces. Each stone was selected, hand carved, and fitted without the use of mortar.

were resistant to earthquakes. This strategy clearly worked, as the walls have survived centuries of natural disasters. However, they are also an expression of the Incan worldview, where stones have special significance to be celebrated with architecture. The Incas extended these architectural and religious beliefs about stone throughout the empire.

The Incas used simple techniques in their stonework. To split a large stone, the Incas would exploit a fissure in the rock using wooden or bronze pliers. For larger stones, often between 40 and 100 tons (36.3 and 90.7 metric tons), the Incas relied on human power. Over prepared roadbeds, teams of around one hundred workers pulled the enormous stones, pooling their power to move the stone over the prepared terrain. To fit stones together, the Incas were willing to be patient, identifying possible combinations to find the right choice. Incan workers used black cobblestones as hammers, carefully varying each swing's angle and power to chip away the rock. Incan masonry constructed this way was put to remarkably complex uses. Based on the motivation to respect natural rock, the Incas combined a wide variety of techniques: fitting stones together, leaving parts of stones uncarved, designing walls that curve, building window-like outlooks, and carving reliefs into the rough and smooth surfaces of rocks. Each of these individual techniques represents a high level of craftsmanship, but when combined in the Incan fashion, the results are nothing short of extraordinary.

Many sacred places in the Incan Empire combined masonry techniques and natural stones in blends that are simultaneously jarring and graceful. Walls of a building will curve in a gentle spiral around a boulder, which may be carved in the shape of a nearby mountain or feature miniature terraces on its face. Wall stones will be fitted between boulders, which are themselves carved into staircases and walls, giving the appearance of a shattered building having melded into a single warped structure. From a few simple techniques—combined with a reverence for the living rock—the Incas filled the empire with impressive stone monuments. This stonework combined a STEM affinity for learning how materials work with a worldview that combined engineering and religious art.

A SACRED RELATIONSHIP WITH STONE

When most structures are built, they are considered nothing but objects. People grind stones and gravel, saw wood, mix cement, and melt steel, without giving them much thought. The Incas, however, did not have the same mindset as modern builders. In the Incan religious system, stones are living beings filled with sacred presence. This conception of stone as alive helped motivate some of the choices Incas made in

The walls of Sacsayhuaman, featuring some combinations of different masonry styles are shown here. Sacsayhuaman was where Cuzco residents would celebrate the holiday of Inti Raymi.

their stonework. For the Incas, sacred stones were the embodiments of mythic ancestors, and stones served as a gateway to another world, where the ancestors still lived. The Tiwanaku people were said to be made of stone, and many stones were seen as petrified forms of ancient ancestors and soldiers. These beliefs encouraged responsibility to the stone, and thus, to the surrounding environment. Incan stonework would fit into natural outcrops, frame them visually, or augment them with carved patterns. Rather than using stone construction projects as a way of conquering their surroundings, Incas practiced building that connected the human, natural, and spiritual world.

INCAN SETTLEMENT PATTERNS, FROM HOMES TO CITIES

The Incas are known for using a handful of architectural techniques that were repeated throughout the regions they conquered. Looking at the archaeological sites of once-independent communities in the Incan state, one sees that the typically round dwellings of non-Incas were replaced with the Incan style soon after conquest. Along with bonded masonry, these homes had rectangular structures and gabled (diagonal) roofs. Doors and windows were typically trapezoidal. Incan communities were often planned by the state, which also took charge of importing labor to build structures in a consistent style.

For urban planning, there was a single model with countless iterations: Cuzco. A long way from its origins as a humble village, Cuzco was built as the symbolic center of the empire and the spiritual center of the world. Historians believe that Cuzco was designed by Pachacuti, the Sapa Inca who helped define the Incan Empire. Carefully planned and constructed over a twenty-year period, Cuzco was designed to frame the core views of the Incan world and was the template for other cities, such as Quito.

Cuzco was divided into sections called *suyus*. Each suyu represented a quarter of the city and a corresponding quarter of the empire. The northwestern Chinchaysuyu and northeastern Antisuyu comprised the upper moiety, or social division of the empire. The southeastern Collasuyu and southwestern Cuntisuyu comprised the lower moiety. Each of these geographic divisions was also a social division, with every member having a defined set of roles based on place of birth.

Like many Incan designs, Cuzco was built into a rugged landscape. Designed in the shape of a puma, it incorporated the land's natural features into its buildings while also redirecting streams into canals for the city's benefit. This city of twenty to thirty thousand people was restricted to nobles and government workers, who followed ritual rules within its walls. Another fifty to seventy thousand Incas lived in the surrounding suburbs. The city had narrow streets and elegant plazas, one of which was filled with sand from the ocean coast—symbolizing a religious connection with the sea. The Awkaypata plaza, used for state ceremonies, hosted mummies of former Incan rulers. Each Sapa Inca built his own palace, which would become a mausoleum after the ruler's death. This meant that the sacred architecture of Cuzco expanded with each emperor's life and death.

The most significant structure in the city is the Koricancha, a sun temple that served as the symbolic center of the city. This temple featured especially detailed stonework, which was often covered in gold and gems. This gold, which was unfortunately stripped from the temple by the Spanish after the conquest, covered the walls in thick plates. The Koricancha was designed for a range of religious rituals, and many surrounding religious sites were oriented to this primary temple. Today, the Koricancha is site of the Catholic monastery of Santo Domingo, which was built by the Spanish to undermine the indigenous worship of Inti after their conquest of the Incas.

INCAN ROADWAYS CONNECT AN EMPIRE

In the present day, all that remains of the Incan road networks are faint outlines of scattered stone. However, at the height of the empire, the roadway networks covered 15,000 to 19,000 miles (25,000–30,000 kilometers). Two parallel north-south highways, in the highlands and along the coast, were linked by more than a dozen east-west roads and smaller footpaths. Spanish colonists traveling the road raved about the impressive architecture, smooth stone paving, and cleanliness.

A short stretch of a famous Incan road is displayed here. Still intact throughout the region, these roads varied in width to fit the forbidding mountain landscape.

In world history, roads often have the effect of creating economic connections, allowing regional goods to travel far beyond their place of origin, and giving people a greater range of foods, tools, and leisure items. The Incan Empire also benefited from this effect. Goods like potatoes, maize, dry goods, peppers, and coca were carried to different ecological zones, diversifying the Incan diet across the empire. However, while other trade routes—such as the Silk Road in Eurasia or the Roman roads in the Mediterranean—were used freely, Incan roads were restricted to state business. This included *chasqui* messengers, royalty, soldiers, and contingents of workers in the mit'a system. The roads were a testament to the ingenuity of the Incan Empire, but were not built for free movement.

Incan roads were also constrained by the natural environment. Incan pack animals could carry only a limited amount of weight—about 100 pounds (45 kilograms)—which meant that the majority of travel was by foot. Furthermore, because of the inconsistency of the terrain, the Incas would not have greatly benefited from wheeled vehicles, which rely on a relatively level surface. Thus, the Incan road looks a bit different from other roads. They varied widely in width, from 3 feet (1 m) to 16 feet (5 m), depending on whether the roads ran through the forbidding Andes or the easier terrain of the altiplano.

Facing one of the most challenging and varied landscapes in the world, the Incas overcame several obstacles. When confronted by wet marshland, they built an elevated causeway over it. When a mountain road ran into solid rock, they tunneled through it, applying their adaptable masonry techniques to cut tunnels up to 65 feet (20 m). When they encountered an impassable stream, they built stone bridges or braided rope suspension bridges over it. The Incas also developed impressive support infrastructure. In areas vulnerable to flooding, the Incas built drainage canals and culverts. The roads were also supported by retaining walls, using stone in the mountain regions and adobe in the valleys and deserts. These innovative practices helped prevent their roadways from being destroyed by rain, earthquakes, or other natural causes.

THE LONGEST GAME OF TELEPHONE

Using the Incan roads, the empire developed a sophisticated form of rapid communication: the chasqui. Chasquis were young, trained runners who were posted along the road. Typically, these runners would be tasked with carrying a verbal message, quipu, or small item. These runners would move messages along on a relay system; after sprinting a number of miles, runners would pass their message to the next messenger on the path. Like the classic game of telephone, but made more orderly by special training and discipline, the Incas used multiple people to ensure a message or item was delivered quickly and—in theory—accurately.

These messengers would work shifts of about two weeks, staying in a roadside hut at night. During the day, the chasquis stood in wait for a possible delivery. This system was remarkably fast; the chasquis' system could help a message travel up to 155 miles (250 km) per day. It is uncertain just how extensive this messenger network was, however. There were certainly chasquis along the main highways, including a link between the major cities of Cuzco and Quito, but the system may not have covered the entire road system.

The roads are also known for their long series of tambos, or rest stops. These tambos were installed in regular intervals of 10 to 15 miles (15 to 25 km), allowing travelers to rest and resupply after a day's journey. The typical tambo was an adobe construction, more practical than the elaborate stonework other buildings boasted. The tambos included lodgings for travelers, corrals for pack animals, and *collcas*, or storehouses. These storehouses often contained food and other supplies in quantities that could last for several years and were precisely accounted for.

As the lifelines of the empire, the roads were pathways for communication, supplies, laborers, and soldiers. They were the physical foundation of the social structure that joined the efforts of subjects all along the Andes, from the rural outposts to the major cities. The structure and purpose of the roads—as well as the elaborate means of keeping them functional—mirror the unique structure of Incan society: precisely organized, fully connected, and with each element fitting into its rightful place.

CHAPTER FOUR

A SACRED CALENDAR OF SKY AND STONE

In the ancient world, the measurement of time was different from how it is today. While modern societies rely on clocks to precisely measure the minutes and hours and calendars to keep track of appointed days and dates, older societies were more limited. Without instruments for measuring time, the default understanding was shaped by the passing of the sun to measure the day, the cycles of the moon to measure the month, and the turning of the seasons to measure the year.

In typical Incan fashion, scientists and mathematicians wanted to devise a ritual and agricultural calendar that would meet the complex needs of the empire, coordinating labor and religious service requirements on a precise schedule. As a result, their calendar was among the most intricate in the Americas. In the process, the calendar combined geography and monumental architecture, agricultural and religious cycles, and precise observations of astronomical data available to them.

SOLAR ASTRONOMY IN THE TROPICS

The Incas, like many contemporaneous societies, made practical use of solstices and equinoxes along with the phases of the moon. They also witnessed and harnessed an event that took place twice per year: the crossing of the sun at the zenith, or center of the sky. These visible phenomena are fairly easy to reckon because at noon on these days, all shadows are their shortest length. The Incas and other tropical civilizations used a complex astronomical concept called the antizenith, or nadir: a date precisely half of a year from the two zenith passages. These dates are not associated with a visible astronomical event. So what is the nadir and what significance did it have?

The answer lies in the specific astronomical features of the tropics, where the sun and stars appear to move differently than in temperate regions. In these areas, constellations rotate closer to the horizon. As a result, traditional astronomy across the tropics has features not typically seen in astronomy to the north and south. One of those features is the antizenith. In a great feat of abstract scientific planning and thinking, the Incas projected a hypothetical opposite date to the zenith passage. The August antizenith corresponded roughly to the beginning of the rainy season. The October zenith and August antizenith were considered dividing points for complementary halves of the year—male and female—with specific tasks devoted to each subdivision.

ASTRONOMY WITHOUT WRITING

The Incas had a 328-day calendar, divided into 12 months of 27⅓ days, plus a 37-day period that was counted but left off the calendar as a period when time did not take place. Why so complicated? This calendar becomes much more intuitive when seen through the lens of the astronomical features it was based on and the social purpose it had. The Incas were careful observers of the sky and identified several important astronomical phenomena that they used to measure the year: the June and December solstices, the September and March equinoxes, and the cycle of the moon through the night sky. These regular events were linked primarily to periods of

The ruins of the Temple of the Sun in Ingapirca, located in present-day Ecuador, are all that remains of a building that was used for astronomical observation, which meant it played a regional role in the ceque system.

planting and livestock shearing, as well as mit'a labor tributes and ritual schedules. The June solstice—which marks the beginning of winter below the equator—was known as Capac Raymi. The December solstice, which marks the beginning of summer, was called Inti Raymi.

In Cuzco, the Incas built pillars, behind which the sun would drop at noon during the solstices. During Capac Raymi, the upper moiety watching from their appointed place in the city could observe the sun drop behind the carefully placed pillars on the other side of the city. During Inti Raymi, the lower moiety would do the same on the opposite side of the city, preserving the dual balance so important to Incan society.

Along with these solar events, the Incas measured time using various conjunctions of the sun, the moon, and the constellation now called the Pleiades, which Incas called Collca. This constellation cycled around a point at the horizon, and its conjunction with the moon marked the division of months. These sidereal months (meaning months based on stars) take place every 27⅓ days. In addition, once per year, Collca would coincide with the rising sun, which was the event marking the new Incan year. Collca also held an additional significance: in the high-altitude growing areas, the Incas developed techniques for using the constellation to predict seasons of drought. If Collca was covered by clouds when it appeared in the sky in late June, it was taken as evidence of a likely drought. Studies of living communities using this technique have proven that it is a remarkably accurate predictor of El Niño, which would have been an extremely useful tool to the Incas.

THE HUACA: NATURAL RELIGIOUS SITES

The huacas were the shrines of Incan religious life. They were carefully chosen sites from the natural world, believed to be fundamental links between the earthly and the spiritual planes. Huacas were typically boulders or unusually shaped trees and were almost always close to a source of running water. These shrines had a complex purpose: they housed mummies as a final resting place for ancestor spirits; they were sites of ritual sacrifice; and they were frequently used for sky watching on sacred appointed days.

Shown here is Huaca de la Luna, a shrine and administrative complex unearthed in 2001. This structure was constructed by the Moche, a tribe absorbed by Incan conquest.

The Incas made sacrifices to "feed" the huacas, and thus establish a link with Pachamama, the Incan goddess of earth and fertility. Water from the flowing stream, blood from an animal (or, occasionally, a human) sacrifice, textiles, or chicha would be offered at these places. Dwellings would be constructed around them for the comfort of the living spirit that lived in the rock. Along with these features, the structures built around huacas often had astronomical significance. Many would sync with June or December solstices. In southern cave huacas, there were carved openings that allowed light from the sun or moon to shine in on certain days, illuminating a sacred altar. All across the Incan Empire, huacas dotted the landscape, marking places of reverence for the natural world and playing a fundamental role in the Incan calendar.

THE *CEQUE* SYSTEM

The Incas incorporated their calendar into the landscape. The Incas built astronomical observation structures around a number of huacas, shrines for offering reverence to a sacred place in the natural environment. These structures were aligned with astronomical events. When the Spanish were visiting Cuzco, they observed that a place called Koricancha had a special significance in the city. To the Incas, it was the center of a system of forty-one *ceques*—lines of demarcation that extended from Koricancha in all directions. Along these invisible lines lay huacas, which totaled to the same number of days in the ritual calendar: 328. It is likely that the Incas had an 8-day week, resulting from dividing 328 yearly days by 41 yearly weeks. By designing the huaca sites to align with astronomical events, the Incas were able to take an abstract thing—the large-scale calculation of time—and make it concretely connected to the landscape. Each huaca represented a day in the calendar, and, in theory, there was always an event to mark that day.

Huacas in the Incan countryside were somewhat simpler than those in the cities, using the natural horizon more frequently than other structures. Rural Incas would choose a mountain peak that aligned with the noon sun on equinox or solstice days, or they would find a special place on the horizon that matched sunrises or sunsets on other days. In this way, remote subjects of the empire had a degree of control over how they measured time, while still remaining synchronized with the rhythms of the capital.

What makes the ceque system even more complex—but all the more interesting—was that the ceque lines also coordinated the labor tribute requirements of the Incas. In the four quadrants of the Incan Empire, people had appointed religious and social roles to play. The ceques further divided those areas and assigned the task of caring for specific huacas to the people living there. With these assignments also came the schedule of the labor tax. Of course, the everyday needs of an empire do not always correspond neatly to remote astronomical events. It is likely that these appointed days, while still significant, were merely a baseline that could be used to schedule any type of ritual or ceremony.

In the world of the Incas, participation in ritual life kept the cycles of the universe in motion. Just as the "feeding" of the huacas sustained the sacred ancestors that still resided in an area, so too did the keeping of the calendar keep the world alive. Such a view makes sense, given that time was measured in cycles of astronomical events, which corresponded so closely to crucial agricultural and weather cycles measured by the Incas. To build a complex organized society on this basis, the Incas chose not to simply create an abstract calendar of identical days, but to build their sacred places into physical reminders of time's passing. The calendar reinforced social responsibility by investing time with physical importance.

CHAPTER FIVE

THE QUIPU, A SPREADSHEET MADE OF STRING

Nearly every technological development in Incan society—even in recognizable fields like architecture and metallurgy—is done in a way that is distinctive to Andean civilization. One technology stands alone, not appearing in any other place in the world: the quipu. The simplest definition of the quipu is a register of quantitative information in a system of tied, knotted strings. These "spreadsheets of string" were created and transmitted all over the empire, accounting for the precise number of any quantity of things produced or used. The quipu is also a reflection of the way the Incas saw the world. Interpreting that world, and the role the quipu played in it, helps broaden historical understanding of how traditional societies conceived of writing and numbers.

THE QUIPU'S BASIC STRUCTURE

The basic structure of a quipu is both simple and complex: there is a single, thick strand of yarn running horizontally, knotted at the left end. From this primary cord, there are also other, thinner strands of yarn hanging downward in parallel rows, called pendant cords. These rows, looking just a little like

This color engraving depicts the quipu as it may have been used. Features like short and long knots, varying colors, and the looped central top cord appear on many quipus currently being studied.

the parallel rows of mountain terraces, are dyed a variety of colors. Each pendant cord has precisely tied knots evenly spaced down the strand, resembling the regularly placed tambos on the Incan roads. Some of the pendant cords have additional cords attached, also knotted. These are called subsidiary cords. The pendant cords hanging from the primary cord are spaced in groups, with distinct spacing between the groups. Each group has an additional cord facing upward, called a top cord. Though it may seem like a piece of art, this collection of strings and cords tells a story—and each of the strings has a specific meaning.

On each quipu, the differences in the placement, color, and knot are organized to present information. The design of the quipu made it possible to present detailed accounts of different categories of things, such as types of soldiers for an army or types of materials for a storehouse, as well as calculating sums. The quipu could also present hierarchical information, especially genealogies of ayllus who wished to see who was related to whom, and how distant they were from the Sapa Inca, the common ancestor.

On the primary cord, the knotted end marks where the interpreter should start reading. On each pendant cord, the number of knots represented a specific number. Different knots (such as single knots, figure-eights, and long knots) marked decimal position along the cord. Quipu makers could record numbers up to six place values—a remarkable accomplishment. From there, the sequence of strings is organized with the most important information on the first few strings.

These would often include a cord marked with the total, summing the number of units being measured, and other core identifiers.

Following the pendant cords that conveyed basic information, the groups of color-coded pendant cords would record more specific categories. For example, a group of four blue cords could represent numbers of alpaca in four specific villages, and a group of four green cords could represent the same for llamas. Subsidiary cords, attached to the pendant cords, could represent how many in each village needed shearing. Top cords could represent llamas for the whole region, with another subsidiary cord showing how many needed shearing overall. The combinations of these cords and knots were virtually endless.

THE QUIPU IN CONTEXT

The skilled workers who made quipus were called *quipucamayocs*. This position was restricted to men, despite the presence of women in other important roles. The average quipucamayoc was a specialist who learned the art over a four-year training period. He was always a prestigious member of the community and likely had increased access to special goods as a reward for his work as record keeper.

Though Cuzco would have the most elite quipucamayoc, there were also regionally and locally designated makers of the quipu. Quipus were not understood by anyone but the people who made them. Thus, the quipu makers would also read them, serving as the verbal interpreters for the string

A drawing by Felipe Guaman Poma de Ayala, a native chronicler of Incan history, this illustration implies that the Incas saw quipus as a form of writing—in other words, a complex and codified method of communication.

communication. When relay runners would carry a quipu from place to place, they were given precise verbal instructions to accompany the quipu, which another quipucamayoc would use as a key to decode the quipu. There are other instances of quipus being best understood in their surrounding context. When people died, they were often buried with a quipu and a variety of other ceremonial objects, which scholars later used to interpret the quipu. As far as scholars understand, the uses of color and placement were not fully standardized, but were instead a matter of local and personal style. These broad differences required further context to be understood, and there are still many unanswered questions about some discovered quipus to this day.

THE CHACHAPOYAS QUIPU: CRACKING THE CODE WITH SPANISH DOCUMENTS

In 1996, several quipus were discovered in Chachapoyas, Peru. The most elaborate featured 762 distinct pendant cords. Though this quipu is not the largest (some examples have more than 1,000 pendant cords), it is among the best preserved and best understood. Quipu expert Gary Urton examined the sections of the quipu, concluding that it most likely

(continued on page 55)

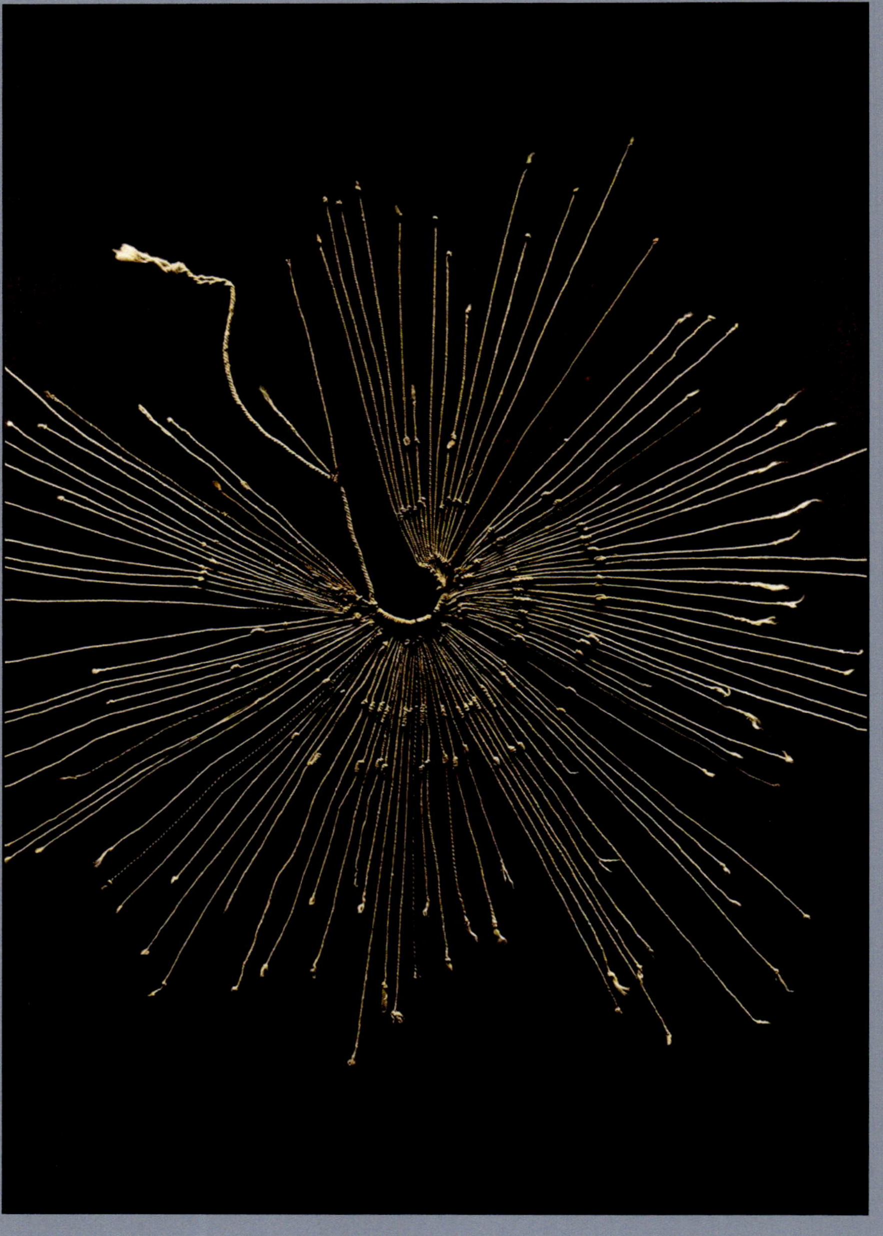

This complex Incan quipu is held on display at the Museum of Pre-Columbian Art in Santiago, Chile. The precise, tight knots reveal the work of a well-trained quipucamayoc.

(continued from page 53)

represented a two-year calendar of mit'a labor. How did he figure this out?

Urton noticed that out of the 762 pendant cords, there are two primary groupings of 362 and 368. Both sets have a further twelve subsections, which mean that they were probably months in a two-year calendar. The years would be uneven because the Incas did not measure the year in the same way as modern timekeepers. The knots in the quipu total to 6,004, thus recording the many acts of labor service by around three thousand people over those two years. According to this hypothesis, each cord grouping supposedly described—by the day and month—who was expected to do what.

UNTANGLING QUIPU MYSTERIES

As an important vehicle for conveying Incan information, many contemporary scholars of the quipu have made significant progress in unraveling their mysteries. These scholars have been able to identify the core means of representing and organizing mathematical information. However, not all of the quipus that have been discovered fit a mathematical pattern. Fully one-third of the existing quipus, instead, have a completely different form of interpretation that has not yet been discovered.

Early Spanish chroniclers observed a different purpose for the quipu, in performers apparently translating some quipu into renditions of epic poems with accompanying dancers. These reports, appearing in many different written sources, would imply that the quipu had elements that could be described as similar to writing. If it were, the quipu would still be unlike any other writing system in the world, but finding out whether it is the case is especially complicated.

Many cultures have different kinds of sign systems, some of which can be interpreted fairly quickly. For example, even though cultures may use different signs for numbers or directions, they are straightforward enough that they can be understood. Written language is different, having to represent a grammar and vocabulary with signs that are standard enough to be understood across gaps of time and space. Because the meaningful features of the quipu—the color, yarn type, and placement—vary from quipucamayoc to quipucamayoc, it is harder to identify what such a pattern would be without some sort of clue. By contrast, even if someone's handwriting is sloppy, it is still understandable because it uses the same symbols and signs as anyone else who knows the same written language.

In the ongoing debate, people have come up with many hypotheses about how the Incas could have represented meaning using the quipu. Some have suggested that combinations of knots represented syllables, or sound patterns. Others have explored the possibility that combinations simply represented chosen meanings or words, similar to a character-based writing system. Both of these scholarly theories have compelling arguments based in their own interpretations of quipus, and some historians are using computers to try to discover hidden patterns in the knotted strings. Modern interpreters have not yet come to a broad consensus, mostly because they have not found a Rosetta Stone of quipus: a quipu alongside a written transcription. What most do agree on, however, is that quipus certainly have extra meaning beyond numbers. In the future, it is likely that historians or anthropologists will discover more about the Incas' unique communication system.

CHAPTER SIX

SPANISH CONQUEST, THE DESTRUCTION AND REDISCOVERY OF INCAN LIFE

In the 1520s CE, the Sapa Inca Huayna Capac began hearing rumors of mysterious bearded, white-skinned men who had arrived in his empire. By 1528, the Sapa Inca had succumbed to one of the illnesses that the Europeans had unknowingly brought with them, ravaging the countryside as it did for many indigenous people of the Americas. In 1532, one of those men, Francisco Pizarro, began a bloody war of conquest that ended with the destruction of the Incan Empire. The end came suddenly and without warning for the Incas.

UNDERMINING THE INCAS FROM WITHIN

Along with the European diseases—to which the indigenous people had no immunity—the Spanish had the technological advantages of steel swords, armor, and various gunpowder weapons. Undoubtedly, these technologies were significant military assets that aided the Spanish against the Incas as they had elsewhere in the Americas. However, it would be a mistake to attribute the defeat of the Incas to those

Francisco Pizarro is most famous as the conqueror of the Incan Empire. In addition to advanced armor and weaponry, Pizarro succeeded by using internal Incan political conflicts to his advantage.

tools alone. The Spanish also arrived at a time of weakness in the Incan Empire.

Pizarro had explored the empire in 1526, and when he returned in 1532, he found a region in chaos. After Huayna Capac died of illness, likely smallpox, there was a war of succession between two of his sons: Huascar and Atahuallpa. Huascar was the oldest and favored by the court, but Atahuallpa had a loyal following in the north and refused to pay tribute to the new king. A civil war broke out, and Atahuallpa defeated his brother and killed him. The ripple effects of this instability led to uprisings by provincial cultures that had resented Incan conquest. These uprisings, combined with civil war and the spread of European diseases, put the Incan state at a significant disadvantage. Though Pizarro had undeniably more effective warfare technology, some historians have claimed that he would have failed to conquer the state at the peak of its power. By the time he set his sights on conquest, however, the Incas' greatest strengths—an orderly society, disciplined culture, and strong central government—had not only vanished, but also turned into the empire's greatest weakness. Pizarro allied with rebelling groups and used Incan collcas to resupply his campaign.

In 1532, the Spanish met with Atahuallpa and proclaimed the empire for the people of the Christian faith. A Spanish Catholic priest met with the Incan ruler and tried to convince him of the power of Christianity, handing Atahuallpa a religious text as "proof" of the faith. Unfamiliar with European writing systems, the Sapa Inca tossed it onto the ground.

Examples of collca storehouses, these structures were excavated in Cochabamba, Bolivia. These storehouses helped Pizarro's troops resupply during his campaign of conquest.

This unintended insult became the pretext for a massacre, in which a small group of Spanish soldiers killed hundreds of Incas before capturing Atahuallpa.

Atahuallpa famously offered many roomfuls of gold and silver as ransom for his freedom. For several months of the Sapa Inca's captivity, his subjects retrieved several tons of precious artifacts, which were promptly reshaped into ingots for shipping to Europe. Though the Spanish thirst for gold would not be satisfied, the conquistadors had already become wealthier than they could have imagined. After the promised ransom was paid, Pizarro had Atahuallpa executed.

After conquering the Incas, the Spanish crown established the encomienda system, which was used across the Americas to force indigenous laborers to work in farms and mines. In the defeated Incan Empire—now the Spanish Viceroyalty of Peru—the Incas' mining skills were put to work in the town of Potosí. Repurposing the mit'a system to create a supply of forced labor, Potosí became one of the most lucrative silver mines in the world, lubricating a world trade of precious metals that reached as far as China. As the Incas rose thanks to STEM, so their world was destroyed by it. Both European technologies and their own turned against them before being nearly erased from history.

THE DESTRUCTION OF INCAN CULTURE

The Incas, watching the Spanish melt their gold and silver, were surprised. Though these metals were of obvious value to them, the act of melting them down effectively destroyed that value. The carefully produced alloys and ritual forms were what made the items significant in the first place—in other words, the metals themselves did not hold value.

This difference of perspective was a prominent characteristic in Spanish encounters with the Incas. Though the Spanish had admired Incan urban planning and infrastructure, they could not understand the worldview that shaped Incan values. As a result, the Spanish systematically destroyed many priceless Incan objects of knowledge and critically undermined a deeper understanding of Incan STEM innovations.

(continued on the next page)

Another archeaological site from the Huaca de la Luna is shown here. As researchers continue to explore Incan ruins, their understanding of Andean life is growing more diverse and complex every year.

(continued from the previous page)

In the earliest years of Spanish administration, they utilized quipus for census taking. After a time, however, they began hunting down and destroying them, obliterating the precise historical records and helping put an end to the practices of the quipucamayoc craftsmen. The Spanish also viewed the huacas through their Christian lens, deeming the sacred spaces heretical and destroying as many as they could. Many Spanish buildings were constructed on top of such sacred sites.

THE ONGOING REDISCOVERY OF ANDEAN LIFE

Though Pizarro had captured Cuzco, the newly established Spanish Viceroyalty of Peru grappled with decades of revolts. Manco Inca Yupanqui, installed as a Spanish-friendly Sapa Inca, grew tired of their abuses and founded a neo-Incan state in the northern region of Vilcabamba. He and his son, Túpac Amaru, waged decades of guerrilla warfare before finally collapsing in 1572. In the centuries that followed, many South American rebels against the Spanish took inspiration from the neo-Incan rebellion, including the successful revolution of Simón Bolívar in the 1830s.

Today, many rural residents of Peru and Bolivia live similarly to the Incas who preceded them. These contemporary indigenous Andean people speak Quechua, the Incan language. They farm and weave textiles using traditional implements. When these people pray, they often recite Roman Catholic prayers blended with traditional Incan concepts, in the same sacred natural spaces as their ancestors.

Many scholars are working to learn the ins and outs of the complex Incan state, continuously revising the Incan body of knowledge along the way. Those who see the Incan Empire as illiterate and warlike are challenged to understand the richness of its religious practices, the low levels of poverty and homelessness, and the conceptual brilliance of the quipu. On the other hand, those who see the Incan Empire as an almost utopian world of communal state support and orderly society are forced to confront the forced labor and frequent resistance to the Incan state.

Instead, surveying all of these facts about the Incas is an invitation into their complex world. Such a world is one of brilliant solutions to a difficult social environment. The Incas coordinated human efforts to build a fully integrated, almost modern world, but used concepts that seem strange from a modern perspective. However, thinking like the Incas—that the culture defined the STEM, which in turn defined the culture—it is possible to find echoes of such lifestyles in the modern world.

TIMELINE

900–200 BCE Early Horizon period, characterized by the rise of the Chavín civilization.

200 BCE–600 CE Early Intermediate period, characterized by the appearance of the Moche and Nazca civilization.

600–1000 CE Middle Horizon period, characterized by the Huari and Tiwanaku empires.

1000–1438 CE Late Intermediate period, characterized by the early Incan consolidation and the presence of smaller states. These states include the Chimú, Chanka, Wanka, Sican, and Colla peoples.

c. 1200 CE The period in which Cuzco is mythically founded by Manco Capac, the first Sapa Inca.

1438–1471 CE The reign of Pachacuti, the ninth Sapa Inca, who launched the rapid expansion of the empire.

1438–1532 CE Late Horizon period, during which the Incan Empire peaked and ending with Pizarro's conquest of Peru.

1463 CE Tupac Inca Yupanqui is appointed head of the army by his father, Pachacuti.

1471–1493 CE The reign of Tupac Inca Yupanqui, who expanded the empire farther north.

1493–1528 CE The reign of Huayna Capac, the last independent Sapa Inca. His death leads to a dispute over succession that causes a civil war over the fate of the Incan Empire.

1519–1521 CE Hernán Cortés conquers the Aztec Empire, founding New Spain. His success inspires Francisco Pizarro's mission to conquer the Incas.

1532 CE Atahuallpa defeats rival Huascar, killing him and becoming Sapa Inca.

1533 CE After Atahuallpa's capture and ransom, Pizarro has Atahuallpa tried and executed.

1537 CE Manco Inca, installed by the Spanish as Sapa Inca, rebels and establishes a neo-Incan state in Vilcabamba, in modern-day Ecuador. It wages warfare against the Spanish for several decades.

1572 CE Túpac Amaru, ruler of Vilcabamba after Manco Inca's death, is captured and executed in Cuzco. Periodic rebellions in his name emerge over the following centuries.

1609 CE Inca Garcilaso de la Vega, a Spanish-educated mestizo, publishes *The Royal Commentaries of the Incas, which* popularizes the story of the Incas.

1911 CE Hiram Bigham, an explorer, discovers and publicizes Machu Picchu for the non-Peruvian world. This discovery sparks a revival of scholarly research into Incan society.

GLOSSARY

aryballos A distinctive Incan pottery style, designed for the easy transport of liquids.

ayllu The Incan family unit; a small group claiming a single common ancestor.

causeway An elevated road or path built on watery terrain.

ceque Geographic lines that divided the Incan Empire into administrative sections. These lines each had a number of huacas, which were used for astronomy, religion, and the organization of social roles.

chasqui A runner tasked with delivering quipus and other messages on the Incan roads. These runners worked in a relay system.

chuño A staple food of the Incas, made of freeze-dried potatoes.

collca An Incan storehouse. Storehouses were an essential component of the economy.

contemporaneous Existing at the same time.

culvert A narrow tunnel redirecting water under a road or path.

cumbi A luxury fabric created by expert weavers. This fabric incorporated a wide variety of materials and was designed for sacrifice, ritual exchange, and social marking.

hierarchical An organizational structure where some things are subordinated to others; common in Incan religion, society, and infrastructure.

huaca A religious site built around a sacred natural space, including mummies and observatories for astronomical events.

huasca An everyday fabric, woven at home and worn by common people.

irrigation The technique of redirecting rivers and streams to be closer to farmlands, making it easier to water crops.

mit'a The Incan system of labor organization. Instead of paying a tax in currency, all Incas were required to supply scheduled labor to the state.

moiety A social division of a population into two distinct groups. Such divisions are common in traditional societies and are often reinforced by parallel religious practices.

phusca A simple handheld spindle, used for producing yarn from cotton and wool.

Quechua The official language of the Incan Empire, adopted by conquered states and still spoken today.

quipu An Incan recording device made of yarn, organizing knots and colors to represent mathematical information.

quipucamayoc A professional quipu maker, trained for the making and interpreting of quipu records.

Sapa Inca The ruler of the Incan Empire and the general term for a common ancestor of an ayllu.

suyu A division of the Incan Empire. The four suyus of Cuzco corresponded to geographic divisions of the empire as a whole.

FOR MORE INFORMATION

American Museum of Natural History
Central Park West at 79th Street
New York, NY 10024-5192
(212) 769-5100
Website: https://www.amnh.org
Facebook: @naturalhistory
Instagram and Twitter: @amnh
The American Museum of Natural History includes collections of Incan art in a wide variety of media. Its website includes further information on Incan crafts.

Ancient History Encyclopedia
Brookhouse Mint Street Godalming
Surrey GU7 1HE
United Kingdom
Website: https://www.ancient.eu
Facebook, Instagram, and Twitter: @ahencyclopedia
This website features articles and entries on countless civilizations, including the Incan Empire, in addition to images and multimedia.

Archaeology Centre
University of Toronto
19 Russell Street
Toronto, Ontario, Canada
M5S 2S2
(416) 978-5248
Website: http://www.archaeology.utoronto.ca
Facebook: @www.archaeology.utoronto.ca
The Archaeology Centre includes information on its archaeological research in northern Peru, focusing on pre-Incan huaca sites associated with the Moche civilization.

Khipu Database Project
Peabody Museum 557A
21 Divinity Avenue
Cambridge, MA 02138
(617) 496-8534
Website: http://khipukamayuq.fas.harvard.edu
The Khipu Database Project includes detailed information on contemporary computer-based research on quipus.

Latin American Research Centre
University of Calgary
2500 University Drive NW
Calgary, AB T2N 1N4
Canada
Website: https://larc.ucalgary.ca
Facebook and Twitter: @LARCCalgary
The Latin American Research Centre offers information on Latin America, past and future. The website includes links to research on the Incas and contemporary Peru.

Michael C. Carlos Museum
Emory University
571 South Kilgo Circle
Atlanta, GA 30322
(404) 727-4282
Website: https://carlos.emory.edu
Facebook, Instagram, and Twitter: @carlosmuseum
The Michael C. Carlos Museum is one of the largest antiquities museums in the United States, with collections including Incan textiles and ceramics. The website includes images of its collections and descriptions of upcoming events.

FOR FURTHER READING

Allan, Tony. *Exploring the Life, Myth, and Art of South America*. New York, NY: Rosen Publishing, 2017.

Croy, Anita. *Who Built Machu Picchu?* New York, NY: Cavendish Square Publishing, 2018.

Day, Meredith. *Revolution and Independence in Latin America*. New York, NY: Rosen Publishing, 2016.

Grafton, Carol Belanger. *Inca Designs*. Mineola, NY: Dover Publications, 2014.

Murphy, John. *Gods & Goddesses of the Inca, Maya, and Aztec Civilizations*. New York, NY: Rosen Publishing, 2015.

Pillsbury, Joanne, Timothy Potts, and Kim N. Richter. *Golden Kingdoms: Luxury Arts in the Ancient Americas*. Los Angeles, CA: The Getty Research Institute, 2017.

Randolph, Joanne. *Living and Working in the Pre-Columbian Americas*. New York, NY: Enslow Publishing, 2017.

Regas, Ricard, and Albert Cañagueral. *The Secrets of Ancient Ritual Sites: The Citadel of Machu Picchu and Stonehenge*. New York, NY: Cavendish Square Publishing, 2018.

Siepel, Kevin H. *Conquistador Voices: The Spanish Conquest of the Americas as Recounted Largely by the Participants*, vol. 2. Angola, NY: Spruce Tree Press, 2015.

Statland-Ellis, Leanne. *The Ugly One*. Boston, MA: Clarion Books, 2015.

Williams, Brian, and Caroline Dodds Pennock. *Maya, Incas, and Aztecs*. New York, NY: DK Publishing, 2018.

BIBLIOGRAPHY

Ascher, Marcia, and Robert Ascher. *Code of the Quipu: A Study in Media, Mathematics, and Culture*. Ann Arbor, MI: University of Michigan Press, 1981.

Aveni, Anthony F. *Empires of Time: Calendars, Clocks, and Cultures*. New York, NY: Basic Books, 1989.

D'Altroy, Terence N. *The Incas*. Malden, MA: Wiley Blackwell, 2015.

Dean, Carolyn. *A Culture of Stone: Inka Perspectives on Rock*. Durham, NC: Duke University Press, 2010.

Julien, Catherine. *Reading Inca History*. Iowa City, IA: University of Iowa Press, 2000.

Magli, Giulio. *Archaeoastronomy: Introduction to the Science of Stars and Stones*. New York, NY: Springer, 2016.

McEwan, Gordon F., ed. *Pikillacta: The Wari Empire in Cuzco*. Iowa City, IA: University of Iowa Press, 2005.

Niles, Susan A. *The Shape of Inca History: Narrative and Architecture in an Andean Empire*. Iowa City, IA: University of Iowa Press, 1999.

Ruggles, Clive, and Gary Urton, ed. *Skywatching in the Ancient World: New Perspectives in Cultural Astronomy*. Boulder, CO: University Press of Colorado, 2007.

Shimada, Izumi, ed. *The Inka Empire: A Multidisciplinary Approach*. Austin, TX: University of Texas Press, 2015.,

Somervill, Barbara. *Empire of the Inca*. New York, NY: Facts on File, 2004.

Suarez, Ananda Cohen, and Jeremy James George. *Handbook to Life in the Inca World*. New York, NY: Facts on File, 2011.

Urton, Gary. *Inka History in Knots: Reading Khipus as Primary Sources*. Austin, TX: University of Texas Press, 2017.

Urton, Gary, and Adriana Von Hagen, ed. *Encyclopedia of the Incas*. Lanham, MD: Rowman and Littlefield, 2015.

Yupangui, Diego de Castro. *An Inca Account of the Conquest of Peru*. Translated by Ralph Bauer. Boulder, CO: University Press of Colorado, 2005.

Zuidema, R. T. *The Ceque System of Cuzco: The Social Organization of the Capital of the Inca*. Leiden, Netherlands: E. J. Brill, 1964.

INDEX